I0821393

# KANSAS CITY CHIEFS

BY TODD KORTEMEIER

SportsZone
An Imprint of Abdo Publishing
abdopublishing.com

abdopublishing.com

Published by Abdo Publishing, a division of ABDO, PO Box 398166, Minneapolis, Minnesota 55439. 

Printed in the United States of America, North Mankato, Minnesota
042016
092016

Cover Photo: Ed Zurga/AP Images
Interior Photos: Ed Zurga/AP Images, 1; AP Images, 4-5, 10-11, 16-17; Tony Tomisc/AP Images, 6-7; NFL Photos/AP Images, 8-9; Rich Clarkson/AP Images, 12-13; Bill Achatz/AP Images, 14-15; Erik Hill/AP Images, 18-19; G. Newman Lowrance/AP Images, 20, 21, 22-23; Tim Johnson/AP Images, 24-25; Greg Trott/AP Images, 26-27; Rick Osentoski/AP Images, 28; Peter Read Miller/AP Images, 29

Editor: Patrick Donnelly
Series Designer: Nikki Farinella

**Cataloging-in-Publication Data**
Names: Kortemeier, Todd, author.
Title: Kansas City Chiefs / by Todd Kortemeier.
Description: Minneapolis, MN : Abdo Publishing, [2017] | Series: NFL up close | Includes index.
Identifiers: LCCN 2015960437 | ISBN 9781680782219 (lib. bdg.) | ISBN 9781680776324 (ebook)
Subjects: LCSH: Kansas City Chiefs (Football team)--History--Juvenile literature. | National Football League--Juvenile literature. | Football--Juvenile literature. | Professional sports--Juvenile literature. | Football teams--Kansas--Juvenile literature.
Classification: DDC 796.332--dc23
LC record available at http://lccn.loc.gov/2015960437

# TABLE OF CONTENTS

Minnesota Vikings defensive end Carl Eller, *81,* bears down on Chiefs quarterback Len Dawson, *16,* in the Super Bowl.

# CHAMPION CHIEFS

The 1969 Kansas City Chiefs were the last champions of the American Football League (AFL). Their league would merge with the National Football League (NFL) in 1970. But first, the two league champions faced off one more time in the Super Bowl.

The Chiefs were facing the NFL champion Minnesota Vikings in the fourth Super Bowl. Even though the AFL's New York Jets had won Super Bowl III, most fans and media thought that was a fluke. The NFL was still considered a much better league.

## FAST FACT

Five Hall of Famers played on Kansas City's defense: cornerback Emmitt Thomas, defensive tackles Curley Culp and Buck Buchanan, and linebackers Bobby Bell and Willie Lanier.

The Chiefs did not buy into that thinking. They believed they were a good match for the Vikings. Their defense was loaded, and it put the clamps on Minnesota. The Chiefs forced five Minnesota turnovers and shut down the Vikings' running game. The Kansas City offense did just enough to take a 16-0 lead at halftime.

Buck Buchanan, *left*, and Curley Culp put the wraps on Vikings running back Dave Osborn in the Super Bowl.

## FAST FACT

Three other members of the 1969 Chiefs were enshrined in the Pro Football Hall of Fame: Len Dawson, kicker Jan Stenerud, and coach Hank Stram.

The Vikings scored late in the third quarter to cut the Chiefs' lead to 16-7. But on Kansas City's next possession, Otis Taylor made the play of the game. The Chiefs wide receiver caught a short pass from quarterback Len Dawson along the sideline. He dodged one Vikings defender and then sprinted 40 yards to the end zone. Final score: Chiefs 23, Vikings 7.

Dawson was named the game's Most Valuable Player (MVP). It was the second championship for the Chiefs, who won the AFL title in 1962 while playing in a different city.

Otis Taylor, *89*, ducks a tackle from Minnesota safety Paul Krause.

Abner Haynes, *28*, carries the ball for the Dallas Texans in a 1962 game against the Buffalo Bills.

**FAST FACT**
The 1962 AFL Championship Game was the longest game in pro football history at the time. It lasted 77 minutes, 54 seconds.

# THE FIRST TEXANS

Dallas businessman Lamar Hunt watched the 1958 NFL Championship Game with great interest. The Baltimore Colts beat the New York Giants in overtime. People from coast to coast watched the exciting game on national television, a rarity at the time. Later called "The Greatest Game Ever Played," it inspired Hunt to try to bring a football team to his hometown.

He failed in his effort to get an NFL team. But he was able to secure a team in the brand new AFL. By their third season, the Dallas Texans were the best team in the league on offense and defense. Quarterback Len Dawson, the AFL Player of the Year, led them to the 1962 AFL Championship Game, where they beat the Houston Oilers 20-17 in double overtime.

## FAST FACT

The Chiefs' first home in Kansas City was Municipal Stadium. They shared it with two baseball teams, first the Athletics and later the Royals.

The Texans may have beaten their competition on the field. But off the field, they could not compete with their crosstown rivals. The NFL's Dallas Cowboys began play in 1960, the same year as the Texans. The two teams even shared the same home field in the Cotton Bowl. Dallas was not big enough for the two of them.

So Hunt moved his team to a city without pro football. After considering Atlanta and Miami, Hunt chose Kansas City. The team picked up a new nickname, but its winning ways did not change.

Chiefs defensive back Dave Grayson, *left*, tries to break up a pass intended for Charley Mitchell of the Denver Broncos in 1963.

KC

# SUPER BOWL SUCCESS

The Chiefs had only one losing season in their seven years in the AFL. In 1966, they went 11-2-1 and won their second AFL title. That earned them a spot in the first ever AFL-NFL World Championship Game, known today as the Super Bowl. Their opponents were the NFL champion Green Bay Packers.

**FAST FACT**

Hank Stram coached the Chiefs from 1960 to 1974. His 124 wins are the most in team history.

Chiefs players carry coach Hank Stram off the field after they defeated the Buffalo Bills 31-7 in the 1966 AFL Championship Game.

Chiefs quarterback Len Dawson, *16*, drops back to pass against the Green Bay Packers in the first Super Bowl.

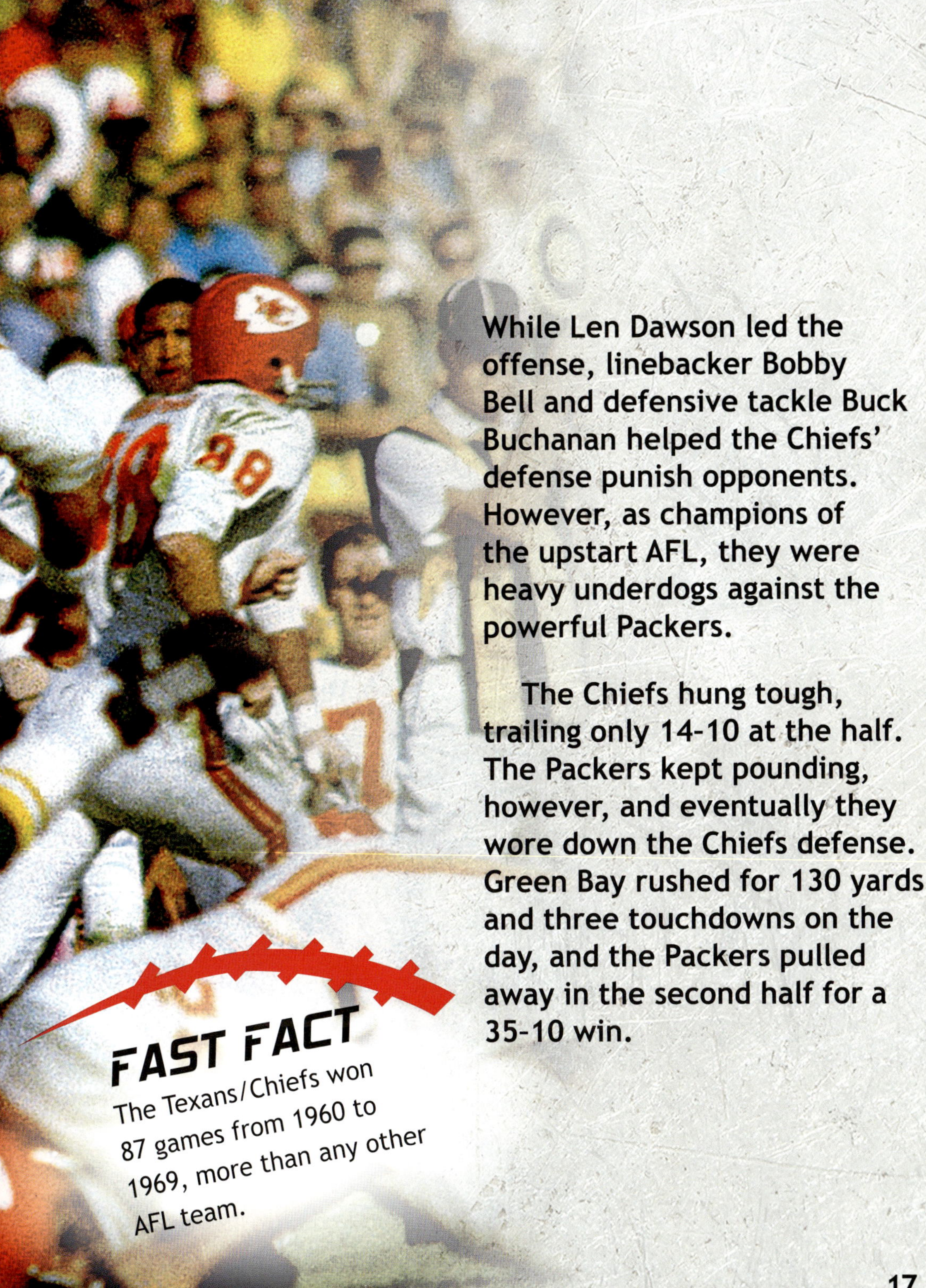

While Len Dawson led the offense, linebacker Bobby Bell and defensive tackle Buck Buchanan helped the Chiefs' defense punish opponents. However, as champions of the upstart AFL, they were heavy underdogs against the powerful Packers.

The Chiefs hung tough, trailing only 14-10 at the half. The Packers kept pounding, however, and eventually they wore down the Chiefs defense. Green Bay rushed for 130 yards and three touchdowns on the day, and the Packers pulled away in the second half for a 35-10 win.

**FAST FACT**

The Texans/Chiefs won 87 games from 1960 to 1969, more than any other AFL team.

The Chiefs went through some lean years after the stars of their 1960s teams retired.

## FAST FACT

The Chiefs lost to the Miami Dolphins 27–24 in double overtime in a 1971 AFC playoff game. At 82 minutes, 40 seconds, it remains the longest game in NFL history.

In 1969, the Chiefs had to prove they could get by without Dawson. While their star quarterback was out with a knee injury, untested backup Mike Livingston sparked a five-game winning streak. The Chiefs got back to the Super Bowl, and this time they took care of business against the Minnesota Vikings in a huge upset.

The next year, the AFL and NFL completed their merger. The Chiefs and their fellow AFL teams joined three other NFL teams in the new American Football Conference (AFC). Kansas City kept winning in its new league, but not for long. After a playoff appearance in 1971, the Chiefs went 14 seasons before their next.

# MARTY AND MONTANA

By 1989, the Chiefs' Super Bowl years were far behind them. They had only been to the playoffs twice since then. No coach had managed to come close to the achievements of the legendary Hank Stram.

That changed with the hiring of coach Marty Schottenheimer. The former AFL Pro Bowl linebacker led the Cleveland Browns to the playoffs four straight years. He had similar success in Kansas City.

Neil Smith, *right*, lowers the boom on Rams quarterback Chris Chandler in 1994.

Linebacker Derrick Thomas was one of the NFL's most feared pass rushers of the 1990s.

**FAST FACT**
The Chiefs drafted defensive end Neil Smith second overall in 1988. They picked linebacker Derrick Thomas with the fourth pick in the 1989 draft.

Running back Marcus Allen carries the ball against the Chicago Bears in 1993.

## FAST FACT

Derrick Thomas's career came to a tragic end when he died following a serious car accident in 2000 at the age of 33.

In 1990, the Chiefs won 11 games, their most since the 1969 Super Bowl year. It was the first of six consecutive playoff seasons. In 1993, they added a pair of former Super Bowl MVPs, trading for star quarterback Joe Montana and signing free agent running back Marcus Allen. The two future Hall of Famers led the Chiefs on a thrilling run to the AFC title game that year.

The fans and media called it "Montana Magic." The former San Francisco 49ers legend led two stunning fourth-quarter comebacks in the playoffs. First the Chiefs beat the Pittsburgh Steelers 27-24 in overtime. Then they scored three touchdowns in the fourth quarter to beat the Houston Oilers 28-20. The magic finally ran out early in the second half of the conference championship. Montana got hurt. The Buffalo Bills were too much for the undermanned Chiefs, and they pulled away for a 30-13 win.

Montana retired after the next season, and Allen retired in 1997. Then it was Schottenheimer's turn in 1998, after the Chiefs went 7-9. It was his only losing season in Kansas City.

## FAST FACT

In 1995, the Chiefs won three games thanks to touchdown returns to the west end zone of Arrowhead Stadium. This end zone was called "Hallelujah Corner."

Joe Montana throws a pass under heavy pressure from Glenn Montgomery of the Houston Oilers in the 1993 AFC playoffs.

Tony Gonzalez, *88*, was one of the best tight ends in NFL history.

# UPS AND DOWNS

The Chiefs drafted tight end Tony Gonzalez in 1997. His size, quickness, agility, and soft hands made him tough to stop. But even with Gonzalez, the Chiefs struggled to find consistent success.

Dick Vermeil started coaching the Chiefs in 2001. He had won the Super Bowl with the St. Louis Rams two seasons earlier. Gonzalez teamed with quarterback Trent Green and running back Priest Holmes in an explosive offense. In 2003, the Chiefs tied a team record with 13 wins. Holmes ran for 1,420 yards and 27 touchdowns. But his 178-yard, two-touchdown performance was not enough to win a playoff shootout with the Indianapolis Colts.

**FAST FACT**

Tony Gonzalez had 10,040 receiving yards in his Chiefs career, the most in team history.

The Chiefs traded Gonzalez to the Atlanta Falcons in 2009. Their next offensive weapon soon emerged. Running back Jamaal Charles was a threat as a runner and receiver. But the Chiefs were not able to translate Charles's blazing speed into playoff wins.

In 2015, Charles suffered a season-ending knee injury in the team's fifth game. The Chiefs started 1-5. With Charles out, quarterback Alex Smith and one of the NFL's best defenses led the Chiefs to 10 straight wins to end the regular season. Then they shut out the Houston Texans 30-0 for their first playoff win since 1994. The Chiefs lost to New England in the next round, but they hope to build on their success and bring a little magic back to Kansas City.

Jamaal Charles breaks loose against the Cleveland Browns in 2012.

Quarterback Alex Smith led the Chiefs back to the playoffs in 2015.

## FAST FACT

In 2014, Jamaal Charles passed Priest Holmes as the Chiefs' all-time leading rusher.

# TIMELINE

## 1960
Lamar Hunt's Dallas Texans take the field in the AFL's first season.

## 1962
The Texans win the AFL championship 20-17 over the Houston Oilers on December 23.

## 1963
Hunt moves the Texans to Kansas City and renames them the Chiefs.

## 1967
The Chiefs win the AFL title on January 1 and go on to their first Super Bowl, where they lose to the Green Bay Packers on January 15.

## 1970
The Chiefs win their third AFL title on January 4 and beat the Minnesota Vikings a week later in the Super Bowl.

## 1994
Joe Montana leads the Chiefs to the AFC Championship Game, but they lose to the Buffalo Bills 30-13 on January 23.

## 2003
The Chiefs tie a team record with 13 wins and score 484 points, the most in team history.

## 2016
After winning their last 10 games of the season, the Chiefs win their first playoff game since 1994 with a 30-0 shutout of the Houston Texans on January 9.

# GLOSSARY

## CONFERENCE
A group of divisions that help form a league.

## DEFENSIVE TACKLE
A player who lines up in the middle of the defensive line.

## DRAFT
The process by which teams select players who are new to the league.

## LINEBACKER
A defensive player who usually lines up behind the defensive line.

## OVERTIME
An extra period or periods played in the event of a tie.

## PLAYOFFS
A set of games played after the regular season that decides which team will be the champion.

## SACK
A tackle of the quarterback behind the line of scrimmage before he can pass the ball.

## TIGHT END
An offensive player who sometimes catches passes but is also responsible for blocking.

# INDEX



# ABOUT THE AUTHOR

Todd Kortemeier has authored dozens of books for young people, primarily on sports topics. He is a graduate of the University of Minnesota's School of Journalism & Mass Communication and lives near Minneapolis with his wife.